THE
ROTTWEILER

by Charlotte Wilcox

CAPSTONE PRESS
MANKATO, MINNESOTA

C A P S T O N E   P R E S S
818 North Willow Street • Mankato, MN 56001

Printed in the United States of America.

Library of Congress Cataloging-in-Publication Data
Wilcox, Charlotte.
    The Rottweiler /by Charlotte Wilcox
    p. cm.--(Learning about dogs)
    Includes bibliographical references (p. 46) and index.
    Summary: An introduction to the Rottweiler, which includes its history, development, uses, and care.
    ISBN 1-56065-395-7
    1. Rottweiler dog--Juvenile literature. [1. Rottweilers dog.]
    I. Title. II. Series:Wilcox, Charlotte. Learning about dogs.
SF429.R7W54 1996
636.7'3--dc20

                                              96-26563
                                                 CIP
                                                  AC

Photo credits
William Muñoz, cover, 8.
Don and Pat White, 4, 34, 38-39.
Reynolds Photography, 6, 13, 16.
Archive Photos, 10.
FPG, 20, 26, 30.
Unicorn, 22; Dick Young, 14, 18, 28, 32, 36, 40; Bob
    Barrett, 24.

Table of Contents

Words in **boldface** type in the text are defined in the Glossary in the back of this book.

Quick Facts about the Rottweiler

Description

Height: Males stand 24 to 27 inches (61 to
           68-1/2 centimeters) and females stand 22
           to 25 inches (56 to 63-1/2 centimeters)
           from the ground to the top of shoulders.

Weight: Males weigh 95 to 135 pounds (43 to 61
           kilograms) and females weigh 80 to 100
           pounds (36 to 45 kilograms).

Physical features: Rottweilers are heavy dogs with small ears folded high on the head. Sometimes they are born with no tail or a very short one.

Color: Rottweilers are black with tan markings.

Development

Place of origin: Rottweilers originated in Germany.

History of breed: Rottweilers descended from the **mastiffs**, which were crossed with herding dogs from around Rottweil, Germany.

Numbers: Close to 100,000 Rottweilers are **registered** each year in the United States. More than 4,000 are registered in Canada. Many more are born every year but are not registered.

Uses

Rottweilers can be trained to do police work, herd cattle and sheep, help disabled persons, guard people and property, and pull sleds and carts.

Chapter 1

The Truth about Rottweilers

Sometimes it is hard to remember what is true and what is false about Rottweilers. Many people think Rottweilers are mean, scary dogs. Movies and television shows often present Rottweilers as bad dogs. Many people think all Rottweilers are angry. But Rottweilers are not like that if they are properly trained. They are dependable and obedient. They like to be with people they love and trust.

Rottweilers are dependable, loving, and obedient if they are properly trained.

Rottweilers are large and protective. They make excellent guard dogs because they are loyal to their families. They make devoted companions. They are active and well coordinated. They help persons with disabilities.

Rottweilers, like any dogs, can become mean and dangerous if they are treated poorly. But most Rottweilers are loving and playful. They should be trained when they are puppies. They should be around other puppies and people. It is important for a Rottweiler to know that its owner is the boss. But it also needs to be treated with love. This will keep the Rottweiler from becoming angry and violent.

Rottweilers are special dogs, and they need special owners. The breed almost died out in the early 1900s. But today, Rottweilers are one of the most popular dog breeds in North America.

Rottweilers will grow up to be better dogs if they spend time with other puppies and people.

Chapter 2

Beginnings of the Rottweiler

Two thousand years ago, the ancient Roman army set out to conquer the world. With thousands of soldiers, it marched across Europe, North Africa, and the Middle East.

One of the biggest challenges was feeding the army. If the soldiers did not get enough to eat, they could not fight. They might even quit their jobs. Rome would lose control.

Feeding the Troops

It was impossible to prepare food at home and haul it hundreds of miles to the army

Rottweilers are descended from the ancient mastiff dogs.

camps. The only means of transportation was slow-moving wagons pulled by donkeys or oxen. With no refrigerators, the food would spoil.

The Romans solved this problem by bringing fresh food along. They called it having food on the hoof. Herds of cattle followed the Romans as they conquered town after town across southern Europe. The cattle provided fresh meat, milk, butter, and cheese. But the cattle did not follow the army on their own. Help was needed to keep them in line.

Drovers and Dogs

The army hired **drovers** to take care of the cattle as they traveled. The drovers' job was very important. They kept the cattle away from the battlefront. They made sure the cows did not run away.

Drovers did not have horses to ride while herding the cattle. The soldiers needed the horses. The drovers needed help driving the cattle on foot. They found the help they needed in the large, intelligent mastiff herding dogs that European farmers used.

Today's Rottweilers are still alert and good at guarding.

Mastiffs are an ancient type of dog known throughout Europe, Asia, and Africa. They were good at hunting, herding, guarding, fighting, and carrying loads. They were everything an army drover needed.

During the day, mastiffs circled the herd and kept it together. They rounded up strays. Some carried packs on their backs or pulled carts of supplies. At night, they guarded the camp and kept the drovers and soldiers company. Some dogs even went into battle with the soldiers.

The Trail to Rottweil

In A.D. 74, the Romans conquered the town of Rottweil, in what is now Germany. After the army left, some Romans stayed in Rottweil. They kept their favorite mastiffs with them.

Farmers around Rottweil liked the mastiffs. They soon started breeding them with their own herding dogs. The result was a muscular dog, a little smaller than the Roman mastiff but quicker and better looking.

These dogs were just as good at guarding the farmer as they were at herding the cows. They were loyal and loving to the family, but they did not trust strangers. Soon farmers from far and near wanted one of the prized Rottweiler dogs.

Rottweilers are loyal and loving to their families.

Chapter 3

Development of the Rottweiler

As centuries went by, Rottweil became a market town. Farmers and their Rottweiler dogs drove cattle into town to sell at the markets. On the way home, the dogs carried the farmers' supplies. Some would even carry the money to keep it from robbers.

The Butcher Dogs of Rottweil

With a lot of cattle in the markets, many butcher shops sprang up in Rottweil. Sometimes butchers went into the countryside looking for cattle to buy. If a butcher bought some cattle, it was his responsibility to get the

Rottweilers were very useful to farmers.

17

Dogs from Rottweil developed tan markings in a special pattern. This made it easy to tell if a dog was from Rottweil.

cattle back to his shop. Soon many butchers started breeding Rottweilers to help them herd the cattle. People began calling them the butcher dogs of Rottweil.

The butcher dogs did more than just drive cattle. They pulled carts of cut-up meat for sale and guarded the butcher shop at night. The butcher dogs worked with people and cattle in this way for more than 1,000 years.

The Rottweiler changed little over the centuries. Owners tried to breed the best dogs. They liked dogs that were smart, dependable, and strong. Rottweilers had to be brave enough to attack a robber or a runaway bull. They had to be gentle enough not to scare the calves. They had to be obedient enough to haul carts of meat without eating it.

Gradually, a favorite color began to appear. Breeders around Rottweil liked black dogs with tan markings the best. Careful breeding produced a pattern. Every dog's colored markings were in the same place. This unique coloring made it easy to tell if a dog was from Rottweil.

When railroads came to Germany in the mid-1800s, farmers began to haul cattle on trains instead of driving them on foot. With no more cattle drives, there was not much need for herding dogs. The Rottweiler breed began to disappear. By 1900, there was only one Rottweiler dog to be found in all of Rottweil.

Making a Comeback

About the same time, Germans began experimenting with dogs for police work. Police officers in Europe and North America already used dogs for tracking, but the idea of a dog and officer as partners was new. Police departments wanted dogs with the right size, personality, and abilities. Rottweilers seemed right for the job.

Soon Rottweilers were members of several police forces. This new career brought Rottweilers to the attention of people all over Europe. It probably saved the breed from dying out.

Rottweilers are very good at police work and search-and-rescue work.

Chapter 4

The Rottweiler Today

In 1901, with very few Rottweilers left in Germany, some Rottweiler lovers formed a club to promote the breed. This club did not last long. But, five years later, a new club began.

The General German Rottweiler Club set up **standards** for how the dogs should look and act. It began keeping **pedigrees** and registering dogs. For a dog to be registered, all of its ancestors must be of the same breed. By 1921, there were 3,400 Rottweilers registered in Germany. People were no longer afraid that the breed would die out.

The Rottweiler is one of the most popular dog breeds in North America.

Rottweilers in North America

The first Rottweilers came to the United States in about 1910. But for a long time most people knew nothing about them. The American Rottweiler Club was not formed until 1971.

Since then, police officers, disabled people, professional trainers, and families have found Rottweilers to be good dogs. The Rottweiler is one of the most popular breeds in North America. Close to 100,000 are registered every year with the American Kennel Club. More than 4,000 are registered with the Canadian Kennel Club.

What Rottweilers Look Like

Rottweilers are easy to spot because of their unique coloring. Their coats are thick and glossy black. The colored markings range from golden tan to reddish-brown. The markings are found over each eye, on the cheeks, throat, chest, lower legs, and on the sides of the **muzzle**. Their almond-shaped eyes are usually dark brown.

Rottweilers are easy to spot because of their markings.

Rottweilers are large, muscular dogs. Males weigh 95 to 135 pounds (43 to 61 kilograms), and females weigh 80 to 100 pounds (36 to 45 kilograms). Males stand 24 to 27 inches (61 to 68-1/2 centimeters) tall, and females stand 22 to 25 inches (56 to 63-1/2 centimeters tall.

Many Rottweilers are born with no tail or very short tails. If a Rottweiler has a longer tail, it is often clipped short.

One of the most pleasing features of a Rottweiler is its calm, confident expression. Triangular ears set high on the nicely shaped head make a Rottweiler look truly noble.

Rottweilers have calm, confident expressions.

Chapter 5

The Rottweiler in Action

One reason so many people want Rottweilers is because they are protective. They have a strong instinct to protect their homes. They show great love for the people they know but will keep strangers at a distance. Sometimes they will use force.

To Protect and Serve

The Germans were the first to train dogs to help in wars. They used such large, protective breeds as Rottweilers, **German shepherds**, and **Doberman pinschers**. Trainers taught the dogs to carry messages and supplies, rescue wounded soldiers, patrol borders, and guard buildings.

Soon police in Germany and England began training dogs to search for bombs and illegal drugs. The dogs were taught to run after criminal

One reason people love Rottweilers is that they grow up to be very protective.

Rottweilers are very protective of their owners and their owners' property.

suspects. They were taught to herd a suspect like they used to herd cattle. Trained dogs will only bark at a suspect who stands still and waits for the officer, but they will attack one who tries to run away.

The police officer's motto is "to protect and serve." This is the Rottweiler's natural desire toward its owner. Police dogs live with the officers and their families, because dogs work best with someone they love and trust. Police work is where Rottweilers really shine. They are so loyal that they will let nothing harm their friend.

One example of such loyalty was a Rottweiler named Bear. She was owned by a deputy sheriff. When a criminal attacked and shot at the deputy, Bear put herself between the deputy and the attacker. She took three bullets to save her owner's life. Both lived to return to work.

Good at Many Jobs

Rottweilers are also popular guide dogs for the blind. Many are service dogs for disabled people, too. A Rottweiler named Eve pulled her owner from a burning van when the owner could not get to her wheelchair. Most Rottweilers never have to save an owner's life, but they do make life easier for a disabled person.

Many people in North America keep Rottweilers as watchdogs or for personal protection. A few lucky Rottweilers still get to herd cattle on farms and ranches.

Chapter 6

A Rottweiler of Your Own

Not every family can provide the kind of home a Rottweiler needs. Rottweilers need a leader. In a pack of dogs, the most dominant dogs fight for the leadership position. The dog that wins is the leader of the pack. This position is called the alpha dog. If there is no alpha dog, Rottweilers feel they must fight to try to win the position.

For this reason, every Rottweiler needs an adult to be its master. The dog must never be allowed to think it can become the alpha dog. Rottweilers can seriously injure people without even trying. Families with children should not bring a new full-grown Rottweiler into the home unless they know for sure that it will accept children it has not grown up with.

Every Rottweiler needs an adult to be its master.

A Rottweiler should have a fenced yard to run in.

Keeping a Rottweiler

Rottweilers need to live with humans. Rottweilers could become dangerous if left in a kennel or alone too much of the time. The best housing for a Rottweiler is in a corner of your house. The area should have a food dish, water dish, chew toys, and a dog bed or cage with a blanket.

Rottweilers need plenty of exercise. Even if you have a yard the dog can run in, you must take the

34

dog walking for at least half an hour every day. Your yard should have a dog-proof fence and a place for the dog to get out of the sun. Rottweilers cannot stand much heat.

To make sure you can find your dog if it gets lost, have your name and phone number engraved on the collar. You could also have a **veterinarian** inject a microchip under its skin. A microchip is a computer chip about the size of a grain of rice. When scanned at a shelter, it will tell the owner's name, address, and phone number.

Rottweilers need obedience training very early. An adult must be the trainer, but the entire family should cooperate. It is very important that young Rottweilers get used to other dogs and people.

Feeding a Rottweiler

Puppies need small meals of good-quality puppy food three or four times a day. They also need plenty of water and a bone to chew. Never give any dog a bone small enough to chew up and swallow. It could get caught in its throat or damage the inside of its body.

By the time a Rottweiler is about one year old, it should have two meals a day of good-quality

The amount of food a dog should eat depends on its size and age.

dry dog food. The amount of food depends on the dog's size, age, and how much exercise it gets. A full-grown Rottweiler may eat two to three pounds (about one kilogram) of dry dog food every day.

Rottweilers need a lot of water. If you cannot have fresh water out all the time, make sure the dog drinks at least three times a day.

Grooming

Rottweilers do not shed much. They are fairly easy to keep clean by brushing them once or twice a week. Dogs should only get baths when they need one. Always use shampoo made for dogs.

Rottweilers have hard toenails that do not wear down easily. If they get too long, the dog can develop foot problems. Trim your Rottweiler's nails often. Take the dog to a veterinarian or professional groomer if you have never done it before.

Clean your dog's teeth often. You can use a soft wet cloth with baking soda on it or dog toothpaste. Never use human toothpaste for a dog.

Health Care

Dogs need shots every year to protect them from serious diseases that can kill them and spread to humans. They also need pills to protect them from **heartworms**. Dogs should get a checkup every year for other worms.

During warm weather, check for ticks. Some ticks carry **Lyme disease** that can cripple a dog

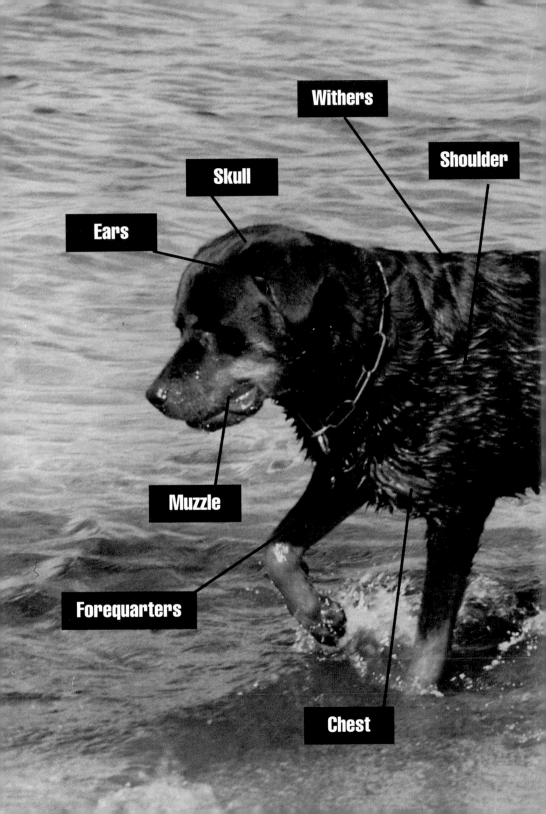

Withers

Shoulder

Skull

Ears

Muzzle

Forequarters

Chest

Tail

Hindquarters

Hock

All dogs need shots to protect them from diseases.

or human. Humans cannot catch Lyme disease from dogs, but they can get it from the tick that bit the dog. Put rubbing alcohol on the tick and pull it out with tweezers. Drown it in rubbing alcohol or bleach. Also check for fleas, lice, and mites.

Where to Get a Rottweiler

A few years ago Rottweilers were a little-known working breed. Now they are one of the most-wanted dogs in North America. Hundreds of thousands have been sold in the last few years. There are many, many Rottweiler breeders. Unfortunately, a few may not care as much about the dogs as they do about the money they get for them. If you want a good Rottweiler, find a breeder who cares about dogs.

A good breeder will not breed a dog with a bad personality or health problems. These traits could be passed on to the puppies. A breeder who cares only about money will use any dog to get puppies, even if they might grow up to be dangerous or unhealthy.

To find a good breeder, contact the Rottweiler club in your area. A good breeder will try to match your family with a puppy that is right for you. Sometimes breeders also have older dogs for sale. They are trained but cannot be used for breeding.

Some Rottweiler clubs operate rescue shelters. They take in dogs that need new homes. Club members can help you find a dog that is right for you. You may find a Rottweiler to take care of that wants to care for you, too.

Dog Facts

Dog Terms

A male is simply called a dog. A female dog is called a bitch. A young dog is a puppy until it is one year old. A newborn puppy is a whelp until it is **weaned**. A family of puppies born at one time is called a litter.

Life History

Origin: All dogs, wolves, coyotes, and **dingoes** descended from a single wolflike dog. Dogs have been friends of humans since earliest times.

Types: There are many colors, shapes, and sizes of dogs. Full-grown dogs weigh from two pounds (one kilogram) to more than 200 pounds (90 kilograms). They are from six inches (15 centimeters) to three feet (90 centimeters) tall. They can have thick hair or almost no hair, long or short legs, and many types of ears, faces, and tails. There are about 350 different dog breeds in the world.

Reproductive life: Dogs mature at six to 18 months. Puppies are born two months after breeding. A female can have two litters per year. An average litter is three to six puppies, but litters of 15 or more are possible.

Development: Puppies are born blind and deaf. Their ears and eyes open at one to two weeks. They try to walk at about two weeks. At three weeks, their teeth begin to come in, and they are ready to start weaning.

Life span:	Dogs are fully grown at two years. If well cared for, they may live about 15 years.

The Dog's Super Senses

Smell:	Dogs have a sense of smell many times stronger than a human's. Dogs use their supersensitive noses even more than their eyes and ears. They recognize people, animals, and objects just by smelling them, sometimes from long distances away or for days afterward.
Hearing:	Dogs hear far better than humans. Not only can dogs hear things from farther away, they can hear high-pitched sounds people cannot.
Sight:	Dogs are **color-blind**. Some scientists think dogs can tell some colors. Others think dogs see everything in black and white. Dogs can see twice as wide around them as humans can because their eyes are on the sides of their heads.
Touch:	Dogs enjoy being petted more than almost any other animal. They can feel vibrations like an approaching train or an earthquake soon to happen.
Taste:	Dogs do not taste much. This is partly because their sense of smell is so strong that it overpowers the taste. It is also partly because they swallow their food too quickly to taste it well.
Navigation:	Dogs can often find their way through crowded streets or across miles of wilderness without any guidance. This is a special dog sense that scientists do not fully understand.

Glossary

color-blind—unable to see colors or the difference between colors

dingo—wild Australian dog

Doberman pinscher—a breed of dog descended from crosses of Rottweilers with racing and hunting breeds; popular as police and guard dogs

drover—a person who herds animals from one place to another

German shepherd—a large breed that is a popular police dog and guide dog for the blind

heartworm—tiny worm carried by mosquitoes that enters a dog's heart and slowly destroys it

Lyme disease—a disease carried by ticks that causes illness, pain, and sometimes paralysis in animals and humans

mastiff—in the past, any large dog used for hunting, herding, or fighting. Today, there are different breeds of mastiffs.

muzzle—the part of a dog's head that is in front of the eyes, including the nose and mouth

pedigree—a list of an animal's ancestors

register—to record a dog's breeding records with a kennel club

standard—a description of the ideal dog of a recognized breed

veterinarian—a person trained and qualified to treat diseases and injuries of animals

wean—to stop nursing or depending on a mother's milk

To Learn More

Alderton, David. *Dogs*. New York: Dorling Kindersley, 1993.

American Kennel Club. *The Complete Dog Book*. New York: Macmillan, 1992.

Day, Alexandra. *Good Dog, Carl*. La Jolla, Calif.: Green Tiger Press, 1985.

Ring, Elizabeth. *Detector Dogs: Hot on the Scent*. Brookfield, Conn.: Millbrook Press, 1993.

Rosen, Michael J. *Kids' Best Dog Book*. New York: Workman, 1993.

Rosen, Michael J. *Kids' Best Field Guide to Neighborhood Dogs*. New York: Workman, 1993.

You can read articles about Rottweiler dogs in *AKC Gazette*, *Dog Fancy*, and *Dog World* magazines.

Useful Addresses & Internet Sites

American Kennel Club
5580 Centerview Drive
Raleigh, NC 27606
E-mail address: info@akc.org
http://www.akc.org/akc/

American Rottweiler Club
960 South Main Street
Pascoag, RI 02859
E-mail address: doreen@ids.net

Rottweiler Club of Canada
2420 42nd Avenue NE
Calgary, AB T2E 7T6
Canada

Kat's Rottweiler Home Page
http://www.in.net/~katl/rottpage/

Rottweilers Reigning Supreme
http://deltanet.com/users/jan4rott/

Brenda's Rottweiler Home Page
http://prysm.com/~im4rotts/stone.html

Index